conte

British & North American Readers:
Please note that Australian cup and
spoon measurements are metric. A quick
conversion guide appears on page 63.
A glossary explaining unfamiliar terms
and ingredients begins on page 60.

on the **side**

Fast and easy, these side dishes are so mouth-wateringly good you'll happily eat them unaccompanied. And each is made using only five ingredients.

almond coriander couscous

2 cups (500ml) chicken stock

2 cups (400g) couscous

20g butter

½ cup (70g) slivered almonds, toasted

2 tablespoons coarsely chopped fresh coriander

Bring stock to a boil in medium saucepan; stir in couscous and butter. Remove pan from heat, stand, covered, about 5 minutes or until all stock is absorbed, fluffing with fork occasionally. **Gently** toss almonds and coriander through couscous.

SERVES 4
Per serving 14.7g fat; 2176kJ

soft polenta with parmesan and sage

1 litre (4 cups) chicken stock

1½ cups (250g) polenta

½ cup (40g) finely grated parmesan cheese

30g butter

2 tablespoons finely chopped fresh sage

Bring stock to a boil in large saucepan, add polenta; simmer, stirring, over low heat, about 5 minutes or until polenta thickens.
Stir in cheese, butter and sage. Serve immediately.

SERVES 4
Per serving 11.7g fat; 1389kJ

buttermilk mash

4 medium potatoes (800g)

4 bacon rashers, chopped finely

⅓ cup (80ml) buttermilk

¼ cup (20g) finely grated parmesan cheese

2 tablespoons finely chopped fresh garlic chives

Boil, steam or microwave potatoes until tender; drain. Meanwhile, cook bacon in small frying pan, stirring, until browned and crisp.
Push potato through sieve into large bowl; stir in hot undrained bacon, buttermilk, cheese and chives.

SERVES 4
Per serving 5.5g fat; 942kJ

4 herbed swordfish
kebabs

You need eight bamboo skewers for this recipe; remember to soak them in water for an hour or so before using to avoid them splintering or scorching.

1kg swordfish steaks

2 medium lemons (280g)

1½ tablespoons finely chopped fresh coriander

¼ cup finely chopped fresh flat-leaf parsley

¼ cup finely chopped fresh chives

Remove and discard skin from fish; cut into 3cm pieces.
Using citrus zester, remove as much rind as possible from the lemons. Squeeze juice from lemons; you will need ⅓ cup (80ml) juice.
Combine fish in large bowl with rind, juice and herbs. Thread fish onto eight skewers; place in single layer in large shallow dish. Pour any remaining marinade in bowl over fish, cover; stand 10 minutes.
Cook skewers on heated oiled grill plate (or grill or barbecue) until browned all over and cooked through.

SERVES 4
Per serving 5.6g fat; 1097kJ

6 ravioli with creamy
spinach and bacon sauce

1kg beef ravioli

6 bacon rashers, sliced thinly

600ml cream

150g baby spinach leaves, shredded coarsely

1 cup (80g) finely grated parmesan cheese

Cook ravioli in large saucepan of boiling water, uncovered, until just tender; drain. **Meanwhile,** cook bacon in large frying pan, stirring, until crisp. Add cream, bring to a boil; simmer, uncovered, about 10 minutes or until thickened slightly. **Add** ravioli, spinach and cheese; cook until heated through.

SERVES 4
Per serving
89.5g fat; 4676kJ

baked **fish** fillets

with cheesy crust

³/₄ cup (75g) packaged breadcrumbs

³/₄ cup (60g) finely grated parmesan cheese

2 teaspoons finely grated lemon rind

30g garlic butter, melted

8 small white fish fillets (1.2kg)

Preheat oven to hot. Combine breadcrumbs, cheese, rind and butter in small bowl. **Place** fish on oiled oven tray; press cheese mixture onto fish. Bake fish, uncovered, in hot oven about 10 minutes or until topping is browned and fish is cooked through.

SERVES 4
Per serving
17.4g fat; 2036kJ

noodles
with chilli chicken

600g hokkien noodles

*500g chicken thigh
fillets, sliced thinly*

*½ cup (125ml) sweet
chilli sauce*

*2 tablespoons
ketjap manis*

*¼ cup coarsely
chopped fresh
coriander*

Rinse noodles under hot
water; drain. Transfer to
large bowl; separate
noodles with fork.
Cook chicken and sweet
chilli sauce in large heated
oiled frying pan, stirring,
until chicken is browned well
and cooked through. Add
noodles, ketjap manis
and ½ cup (125ml) water;
cook, stirring, until heated
through. Remove pan from
heat; toss through coriander.

SERVES 4
Per serving 10.4g fat; 1639kJ

honey mustard
veal chops

*3 large brown onions
(600g), sliced thinly*

*2 tablespoons
brown sugar*

*4 (800g) veal
loin chops*

¹/₃ cup (115g) honey

*¹/₄ cup (70g)
dijon mustard*

Cook onion in large
heated oiled frying pan,
stirring, until soft. Add
sugar; cook, stirring,
until onion is browned.
Remove onion mixture
from pan, cover to
keep warm.
Place veal with
combined honey and
mustard in same pan;
cook, uncovered, about
10 minutes or until
veal is browned both
sides and cooked as
desired. Serve veal with
onion mixture.

SERVES 4
Per serving 5.3g fat; 1674kJ

chorizo tortilla

2 tablespoons olive oil

1 large potato (300g), chopped coarsely

1/2 cup (60g) frozen peas, thawed

100g chorizo sausage, chopped coarsely

8 eggs

Heat oil in 20cm non-stick frying pan; cook potato, stirring, until almost tender, drain on absorbent paper.

Drain excess oil from pan. Return potato to pan with peas and sausage. Beat eggs lightly with 2 tablespoons of water, then pour over the potato mixture in pan.

Cook, covered, over low heat, about 10 minutes or until almost set. Cook under heated grill until tortilla is browned lightly and set. Turn onto serving plate.

SERVES 4
Per serving 26.7g fat; 1509kJ

chicken

and asparagus

green curry

2 tablespoons green curry paste

750g chicken thigh fillets,
sliced thinly

1²/₃ cups (400ml) coconut milk

250g asparagus, chopped coarsely

¹/₄ cup firmly packed
fresh coriander leaves

Cook paste and chicken in large
frying pan, stirring, until chicken is
cooked through. Add coconut milk
and asparagus, bring to a boil;
simmer, uncovered, until asparagus
is just tender.
Remove pan from heat, stir in half
of the coriander. Serve sprinkled
with remaining coriander.

SERVES 4
Per serving 37.8g fat; 2136kJ

chicken with

char-grilled capsicum seasoning

1/3 cup (55g) finely chopped seeded black olives

1/2 cup (100g) sliced, drained, char-grilled capsicums in oil

160g fetta cheese, crumbled

4 (1kg) single chicken breasts on bone

2 tablespoons garlic olive oil

Preheat oven to moderate. Combine olives, capsicum and cheese in small bowl. Push capsicum mixture under skin of chicken, press down evenly. Secure skin to flesh with toothpicks. **Place** chicken, skin-side up, in baking dish; brush with oil. Bake, uncovered, in moderate oven about 40 minutes or until chicken is browned and cooked through. Remove toothpicks to serve.

SERVES 4
Per serving 39.4g fat; 2318kJ

bean and potato
bake

*4 small potatoes
(480g), sliced thinly*

*2 green onions,
sliced thinly*

*1/2 x 220g can
Mexicana chilli beans*

*1/2 cup (125ml)
skim milk*

*1/4 cup (20g)
finely grated
parmesan cheese*

Preheat oven to moderate. Layer potato, onion
and beans in two lightly greased 1-cup (250ml)
ovenproof dishes.
Pour milk over vegetables; sprinkle with cheese.
Bake, uncovered, in moderate oven about
25 minutes or until vegetables are soft.

SERVES 2
Per serving 3.8g fat; 1008kJ

tomato chilli
prawns

24 large uncooked prawns (1kg)

¼ cup (60ml) olive oil

1 medium brown onion (150g), chopped finely

3 large tomatoes (750g), seeded, chopped finely

2 red thai chillies, chopped finely

Shell and devein prawns, leaving tails intact. Heat
1 tablespoon of the oil in large frying pan; cook prawns,
in batches, until just changed in colour.
Meanwhile, heat half of the remaining oil in medium
saucepan; cook onion, stirring, until soft. Add tomato
and chilli; cook, stirring, until tomato begins to soften.
Return prawns to large frying pan with tomato mixture; cook,
stirring, until heated through. Stir through remaining oil.

SERVES 4
Per serving 14.6g fat; 1125kJ

chickpea

and tomato salad

4 medium tomatoes (760g), seeded, chopped

400g can chickpeas, rinsed, drained

$1/2$ small red onion (50g), chopped

$3/4$ cup finely chopped fresh flat-leaf parsley

2 tablespoons lemon juice

Combine tomato, chickpeas, onion and parsley in large bowl. **Drizzle** with lemon juice; season with coarsely ground black pepper, if desired.

SERVES 4
Per serving
1.6g fat; 408kJ

18 char-grilled
steak
with garlic anchovy butter

4 (800g) beef scotch
fillet steaks

90g garlic butter, softened

1 tablespoon finely chopped
fresh chives

1 tablespoon
seeded mustard

2 drained anchovy fillets,
chopped finely

Cook beef on heated
oiled grill plate (or grill or
barbecue) until browned
both sides and cooked
as desired.
Meanwhile, combine
remaining ingredients in
small bowl. Serve beef
topped with butter mixture.

SERVES 4
Per serving 30.1g fat; 1822kJ

spaghetti
with burnt butter sauce

500g spaghetti

125g butter

*2 cloves garlic,
crushed*

*freshly ground
black pepper*

*¾ cup (75g)
coarsely grated
hard goat cheese*

Cook pasta in large saucepan of boiling
water, uncovered, until just tender; drain.
Meanwhile, heat butter in large frying pan,
stirring, until browned lightly. Remove pan from
heat, stir in garlic and pepper to taste. Toss
hot pasta with butter mixture and two-thirds of
the cheese. Sprinkle with remaining cheese.

SERVES 4
Per serving 30g fat; 2856kJ

fish pieces
in beer batter

4 (800g) white
fish fillets

1 cup (150g)
plain flour

1¼ cups (310ml) beer

vegetable oil,
for deep-frying

1 cup (250ml)
tartare sauce

Cut fish into 4cm
pieces. Whisk flour
and beer in medium
bowl until smooth.
Cover; refrigerate
20 minutes.
Dip fish pieces in
batter. Heat oil in
large saucepan;
deep-fry fish pieces,
in batches, until
browned all over and
cooked through. Drain
on absorbent paper.
Serve fish pieces
with tartare sauce
and lemon wedges,
if desired.

SERVES 4
Per serving
36.6g fat; 2767kJ

chicken and spinach
risotto

*1.5 litres (6 cups)
chicken stock*

*2 cups (400g)
arborio rice*

*2 cups (340g)
coarsely chopped
cooked chicken*

*100g baby
spinach leaves*

*1 cup (80g) finely
grated parmesan
cheese*

Bring stock to a boil in medium saucepan, cover; keep hot.
Cook rice in large heated oiled saucepan, stirring, until coated in oil. Add stock, in 1-cup batches, stirring, until absorbed after each addition. Total cooking time should be about 35 minutes or until rice is just tender.
Stir in chicken, spinach and cheese; cook, stirring, until spinach is just wilted. Serve topped with parmesan cheese flakes, if desired.

SERVES 4
Per serving 12.3g fat; 2361kJ

teriyaki **pork** stir-fry

750g pork fillets, sliced thinly

6 green onions, chopped finely

1 clove garlic, crushed

3 (450g) baby bok choy, chopped coarsely

⅓ cup (80ml) teriyaki marinade

Cook pork, in batches, in heated oiled wok or large frying pan, until browned all over and cooked through; remove from wok.
Cook onion and garlic in same wok, stirring, until fragrant. Return pork to wok with bok choy; cook, stirring, until bok choy is wilted.
Add marinade; cook until heated through.

SERVES 4
Per serving
4.6g fat; 959kJ

mint and lime lamb

2 medium limes (160g)

1/2 cup (125ml)
olive oil

2 cloves garlic,
crushed

2 tablespoons finely
chopped fresh mint

8 (1kg) lamb
loin chops

Grate rind finely from limes and squeeze juice; you will need 2 teaspoons of rind and 2 tablespoons of juice. Combine rind, juice, oil, garlic and mint in medium bowl, add lamb; mix well. Cover; stand 10 minutes. **Cook** lamb on heated oiled grill plate (or grill or barbecue) until browned both sides and cooked as desired.

SERVES 4
Per serving
53.8g fat; 2659kJ

cheesy bacon
and egg pie

*2¹/₂ sheets ready-rolled
puff pastry*

*6 bacon rashers,
chopped finely*

*6 green onions,
chopped finely*

9 eggs

*1 cup (125g) coarsely
grated cheddar cheese*

Halve the half-sheet of pastry lengthways;
attach to one of the remaining whole sheets
on adjacent sides; seal joins together with
palette knife. Ease into oiled 23cm shallow
pie dish gently; trim around edge.
Cook bacon in medium frying pan, stirring,
until crisp. Add onion; cook, stirring, until soft.
Preheat oven to hot. Whisk one of the eggs in
small bowl until combined; set aside.
Break one of the remaining eggs in a cup, gently
pour unbeaten egg into pastry case. Repeat with
remaining eggs. Top with bacon mixture and
cheese. Brush edges with beaten egg; place
remaining pastry sheet over pie, trim then press
around edge with fork to seal. Brush top of pie
with beaten egg. Bake, uncovered, in hot oven
20 minutes, reduce heat to moderate; bake
about 15 minutes or until pastry is browned.

SERVES 4
Per serving 32.9g fat; 1998kJ

28 pasta with salami
and char-grilled vegetables

500g spaghetti

200g thinly sliced
spicy salami, halved

2 x 280g jars antipasto
char-grilled vegetables

200g baby
spinach leaves

1 cup (80g) parmesan
cheese flakes

Cook pasta in large saucepan of boiling water, uncovered, until just tender; drain.
Meanwhile, cook salami in large frying pan until crisp; drain on absorbent paper.
Drain vegetables; reserve ¼ cup (60ml) of oil. Chop vegetables coarsely; in same pan, cook vegetables and reserved oil until hot.
Toss hot pasta with vegetable mixture, salami, spinach and half of the cheese. Top with remaining cheese.

SERVES 4
Per serving
30.5g fat; 3262kJ

japanese-style
chicken kebabs

You need eight bamboo skewers for this recipe; remember to soak them in water for an hour or so before using to avoid them splintering or scorching.

500g chicken breast fillets

1/3 cup (80ml) sukiyaki sauce

1 clove garlic, crushed

2 teaspoons grated fresh ginger

1/2 teaspoon wasabi paste

Cut chicken into 3cm cubes. Thread chicken onto eight skewers.

Combine 1 tablespoon of the sauce with garlic, ginger and paste in shallow dish; add skewers, turn skewers to coat well. Cover; stand 10 minutes.

Cook skewers on heated oiled grill plate (or grill or barbecue) until browned all over and cooked through. Brush with remaining sauce during cooking.

SERVES 4
Per serving 6.9g fat; 749kJ

sweet chilli
beef ribs

1.5kg beef spare ribs

*½ cup (125ml)
sweet chilli sauce
with ginger*

*1 tablespoon
soy sauce*

*¼ cup (60ml)
rice wine*

*2 tablespoons finely
chopped fresh coriander*

Preheat oven to moderately hot.
Place beef in large shallow
dish with combined remaining
ingredients, cover; stand
10 minutes.
Place ribs on wire racks over
oven trays, brush with any
marinade. Bake, uncovered,
in moderately hot oven about
30 minutes or until browned all
over and cooked as desired.

SERVES 4
Per serving 11.2g fat; 1270kJ

pizza made easy

A popular favourite, piping hot pizza solves the "What's for dinner?" dilemma. As it's so remarkably easy to prepare, this dinner will be on the table before the hordes even realise they're hungry!

2 x 26cm prepared pizza bases

½ cup (140g) tomato paste

vegetarian topping

3 cups (375g) grated pizza cheese

2 x 280g jars antipasto char-grilled vegetables, drained, sliced thinly

1 cup (160g) kalamata olives

prawn, fetta and basil topping

500g medium uncooked prawns, shelled, halved lengthways

375g fetta cheese, crumbled

½ cup loosely packed fresh baby basil leaves

bocconcini, char-grilled capsicum and salami topping

150g thinly sliced spicy salami

300g baby bocconcini cheese, sliced thickly

1 cup (200g) drained char-grilled capsicums in oil, sliced thickly

spinach and chicken topping

200g mozzarella cheese, sliced thinly

75g baby spinach leaves, shredded coarsely

2 cups (340g) coarsely chopped cooked chicken

Preheat oven to very hot. Place pizza bases on oiled oven trays; spread with paste. Use desired topping; bake, uncovered, in very hot oven about 10 minutes or until base is crisp and topping browned.

Vegetarian topping
Top prepared pizza bases with half of the cheese, then vegetables and olives; sprinkle with remaining cheese.

Prawn, fetta and basil topping
Top prepared pizza bases with prawns and cheese. Sprinkle cooked pizzas with basil to serve.

Bocconcini, char-grilled capsicum and salami topping
Top prepared pizza bases with salami, then cheese and capsicum.

Spinach and chicken topping
Top prepared pizza bases with cheese, then spinach and chicken.

ALL PIZZAS SERVE 4

Per serving vegetarian
29g fat; 3042kJ
Per serving prawn, fetta and basil
26.7g fat; 2788kJ
Per serving bocconcini, capsicum and salami 31.3g fat; 2849kJ
Per serving spinach and chicken
22g fat; 2692kJ

chicken breasts

with citrus glaze

3 medium
oranges (720g)

1 tablespoon olive oil

4 (680g) single
chicken breast fillets

1/2 cup (125ml)
chicken stock

1/2 cup (170g) sweet
orange marmalade

Using a vegetable peeler, cut strips of rind from one orange.
Remove and discard white pith. Cut strips into matchstick-size
pieces. Squeeze juice from oranges; you will need 1 cup (250ml).
Heat oil in large frying pan; cook chicken until browned
both sides. Reduce heat; cook, covered, until chicken is
cooked through. Remove from pan, cover to keep warm.
Add juice, stock and marmalade to same pan; stir over heat
until marmalade melts. Add rind, bring to a boil; simmer,
stirring, about 10 minutes or until thickened slightly.
Return chicken to pan, coat with glaze.

SERVES 4
Per serving 14g fat; 1717kJ

vegetable

pesto pastries

2 sheets ready-rolled butter puff pastry, thawed

1/2 cup (130g) sun-dried tomato pesto

280g jar antipasto char-grilled vegetables

6 medium egg tomatoes (450g)

150g fetta cheese

Preheat oven to very hot. Cut pastry in half. Place the four pastry pieces on two oven trays. Fold pastry edges in to make a 1cm border. Spread pesto over centre of pastry. **Drain** vegetables; pat dry with absorbent paper. Cut vegetables into strips. Slice tomatoes lengthways. Arrange tomatoes and vegetables on pastry pieces; sprinkle with crumbled cheese. Bake, uncovered, in very hot oven 10 minutes. Swap shelf position of trays; bake 10 minutes or until pastry is puffed and browned. To serve, top with small basil leaves, if desired.

SERVES 4
Per serving 36.4g fat; 2262kJ

prawn and
noodle salad

400g udon noodles

*1kg large
cooked prawns*

*¼ cup (60ml) sweet
chilli sauce*

¼ cup (60ml) lime juice

*¼ cup firmly packed
fresh coriander leaves*

Cook noodles in large
saucepan of boiling
water, uncovered,
until just tender, drain.
Rinse noodles under
cold water; drain.
Shell and devein
prawns, leaving tails
intact. Combine noodles
with prawns and
remaining ingredients
in large bowl.

SERVES 4
Per serving 2.3g fat; 1942kJ

lemon and herb
chicken

1/3 cup (80ml) lemon juice

2 tablespoons finely chopped fresh chives

2 teaspoons finely chopped fresh rosemary

2 cloves garlic, crushed

4 (680g) single chicken breast fillets

Combine juice, herbs, garlic and chicken in large bowl, cover; stand 10 minutes. Drain chicken over medium bowl, reserve marinade.
Cook chicken on heated oiled grill plate (or grill or barbecue) until browned both sides and cooked through, brushing with reserved marinade occasionally during cooking.

SERVES 4
Per serving 9.4g fat; 993kJ

balsamic
and ginger beef

*1/2 cup (125ml)
olive oil*

*1/4 cup (60ml)
balsamic vinegar*

*1 tablespoon grated
fresh ginger*

*1 teaspoon
brown sugar*

*4 thick T-bone steaks
(2kg), with fillet in*

Combine oil, vinegar, ginger and sugar in jar; shake well. Reserve
1/4 cup (60ml) of the vinegar mixture; brush steaks all over using
about half of remaining mixture. Cover; stand 10 minutes.
Preheat oven to moderate. Cook beef on heated oiled grill plate
(or grill or barbecue) until browned both sides. Place beef on
oven tray; cook, uncovered, in moderate oven about 15 minutes
or until cooked as desired, brushing occasionally with remaining
vinegar mixture. Remove beef from oven, cover; stand 10 minutes.
Just before serving, pour reserved vinegar mixture over beef.

SERVES 4
Per serving 41.3g fat; 2699kJ

asian chicken
soup with
choy sum

*1.5 litres (6 cups)
chicken stock*

*4 (680g) single
chicken breast fillets,
sliced thickly*

*2 tablespoons
soy sauce*

*100g dried rice
stick noodles*

*300g baby choy sum,
chopped coarsely*

Bring stock to a boil in large
saucepan, add chicken;
simmer, uncovered, about
5 minutes or until chicken
is just cooked through.
Add sauce and noodles;
simmer, uncovered, about
5 minutes or until noodles
are just tender. Add choy
sum; simmer, uncovered,
until choy sum is just tender.

SERVES 4
Per serving 11.4g fat; 1493kJ

tandoori

lamb cutlets

1 medium lime (80g)

12 (780g) lamb cutlets

*¼ cup (75g)
tandoori paste*

¼ cup (70g) yogurt

*2 teaspoons
brown sugar*

Grate rind finely from lime and squeeze juice; you will need 1 teaspoon rind and 1 tablespoon of juice.
Place lamb cutlets in large bowl with combined rind, juice, paste, yogurt and sugar. Cover; stand 10 minutes.
Drain lamb; discard marinade. Cook lamb on heated oiled grill plate (or grill or barbecue) until browned both sides and cooked as desired.

SERVES 4
Per serving
20.2g fat; 1195kJ

chicken schnitzel
burgers

vegetable oil, for shallow-frying

4 (600g) pieces crumbed chicken breast schnitzels

4 hamburger buns

2 medium avocados (500g), sliced thickly

1/3 cup (100g) dijonnaise

Heat oil in large frying pan; shallow-fry chicken until browned both sides and cooked through, drain on absorbent paper.
Split buns; toast until browned lightly. Top buns with chicken, avocado, dijonnaise, and rocket or lettuce, if desired; replace tops.

SERVES 4
Per serving 54.3g fat; 3339kJ

spicy plum-glazed
chicken wings

12 large chicken wings (1.5kg)

1 cup (250ml) oriental plum sauce

2 tablespoons soy sauce

2 tablespoons sweet chilli sauce

35g packet salt-reduced french onion soup mix

Preheat oven to hot. Combine ingredients in large bowl.
Place chicken mixture in large oiled non-stick baking dish. Bake, uncovered, in hot oven, about 30 minutes or until browned and cooked through, turning chicken occasionally.

SERVES 4
Per serving
7.3g fat; 1412kJ

mexican-style barbecued
sausages

8 thick beef
sausages (920g)

1 cup (125g) grated
pizza cheese

$1/2$ cup (125ml) chunky
tomato salsa

$1/2$ medium avocado
(125g), sliced thinly

$1/4$ cup (60g)
sour cream

Barbecue (or grill or
char-grill) sausages
until browned all over
and cooked through.
Cut a slit down
the length of each
sausage, not
cutting through.
Top sausages with
cheese, half of the
salsa and avocado.
Serve topped with
sour cream and
remaining salsa.

SERVES 4
Per serving
76.2g fat; 3578kJ

fish fillets with garlic and chilli

1/3 cup (80ml) garlic olive oil

4 blue-eye fish fillets with skin on (800g)

1 1/2 tablespoons white vinegar

1 teaspoon dried chilli flakes

2 tablespoons coarsely chopped fresh flat-leaf parsley

Heat 1 tablespoon of the oil in large frying pan; cook fish, skin-side down, until browned well. Turn fish and cook until browned and just cooked through. **Meanwhile**, place the remaining oil, vinegar, chilli and parsley in small saucepan; stir over low heat until just warm. Spoon oil mixture over the fish.

SERVES 4
Per serving 22.7g fat; 367kJ

chicken with
mango salsa

1 cooked chicken

*1 medium mango
(430g), chopped finely*

*1 small red onion
(100g), chopped finely*

*1 medium avocado
(250g), chopped finely*

*¼ cup (60ml) bottled
french salad dressing*

Cut the chicken into
large pieces.
Combine remaining
ingredients in medium
bowl, mix gently.
Serve the chicken
with mango salsa.

SERVES 4
Per serving
46.1g fat; 2749kJ

baked pasta

with mushrooms

*We used a mixture of mushrooms in this recipe. You can use one variety
or any selection, including swiss brown, button, oyster, flat and enoki.*

500g penne

2 tablespoons olive oil

500g mixed
mushrooms,
sliced thinly

750g tomato
pasta sauce

2 cups (250g) grated
pizza cheese

Preheat oven to moderate. Oil deep 3-litre (12-cup)
ovenproof dish. Cook pasta in large saucepan of boiling
water, uncovered, until just tender, drain. Do not rinse.
Heat oil in large frying pan; cook mushrooms, stirring,
until tender and browned lightly. Place half of the pasta
over base of prepared dish. Top with half of the pasta
sauce and half of the mushrooms and cheese. Repeat
layers with remaining pasta, pasta sauce, mushrooms
and cheese. Bake, uncovered, in moderate oven about
25 minutes or until browned lightly and heated through.

SERVES 4
Per serving 25.9g fat; 3389kJ

rack of **lamb**
with chilli-orange glaze

*1/2 cup (125ml)
orange juice*

*1/2 cup (170g) sweet
orange marmalade*

*2 tablespoons mild
chilli sauce*

*2 tablespoons
seeded mustard*

*2 racks of lamb,
with 6 cutlets each*

Preheat oven to moderate.
Combine juice, marmalade, sauce
and mustard in small saucepan.
Bring to a boil; remove from heat.
Place lamb in large oiled baking
dish; pour over hot glaze. Bake,
uncovered, in moderate oven
about 40 minutes or until lamb
is browned and cooked as
desired, spooning glaze over
lamb occasionally.

SERVES 4
Per serving 19.8g fat; 1658kJ

pumpkin gnocchi
with olives and fetta

1kg pumpkin gnocchi

200g jar sun-dried tomatoes, in oil

1 cup (160g) kalamata olives

375g fetta cheese, chopped coarsely

1/3 cup finely shredded fresh basil

Cook gnocchi in large saucepan of boiling water, uncovered, until just tender; drain. **Drain** tomatoes, reserve 2 tablespoons of the oil. Heat tomatoes and reserved oil in large frying pan, add gnocchi, olives, cheese and basil; cook, tossing gently, until just heated through.

SERVES 4
Per serving
41.8g fat; 4157kJ

easy lasagne

750g minced beef

600g tomato pasta sauce

4 cups (800g) ricotta cheese

3 cups (240g) finely grated parmesan cheese

12 (200g) instant lasagne pasta sheets

Preheat oven to hot. Cook beef in large heated oiled frying pan, stirring, until browned well. Add sauce, bring to a boil. **Combine** ricotta with 2 cups of the parmesan. Spoon a third of beef mixture over base of oiled shallow 2.5-litre (10-cup) ovenproof dish. Top with four of the pasta sheets and a quarter of the cheese mixture. Top with another third of the beef mixture, another four pasta sheets and another quarter of the cheese mixture, then remaining beef mixture. **Top** with remaining pasta sheets; spread over remaining cheese mixture. Bake, covered, in hot oven about 35 minutes or until pasta is tender. Sprinkle with remaining parmesan; cook under heated grill until cheese is browned.

SERVES 4
Per serving 57.7g fat; 4492kJ

fish with
teriyaki chilli sauce

*1 tablespoon
peanut oil*

*4 white fish
cutlets (1kg)*

*1/3 cup (80ml)
teriyaki marinade*

*1 tablespoon sweet
chilli sauce*

*4 green onions,
sliced thinly*

Heat oil in large
frying pan; cook fish
until browned both
sides and just cooked
through. Remove
fish from pan, cover
to keep warm.
Add marinade and
sauce to pan; cook,
stirring, until hot.
Serve fish with
sauce, topped with
green onions.

SERVES 4
Per serving
8.6g fat; 934kJ

green **peppercorn**
and mustard pork

¼ cup (70g)
seeded mustard

2 cloves garlic,
crushed

2 tablespoons drained
green peppercorns,
chopped finely

4 (800g) pork
leg steaks

2 tablespoons
balsamic vinegar

Rub mustard, garlic and peppercorns over
both sides of pork. Cook pork, in batches,
in large heated oiled frying pan, until browned
both sides and cooked through. Remove
pork from pan, cover to keep warm.
Add vinegar to pan, bring to a boil;
remove from heat. Serve pork drizzled
with vinegar mixture.

SERVES 4
Per serving 8.4g fat; 1120kJ

barbecued
thai-style prawns

24 large uncooked prawns (1kg)

3 cloves garlic, crushed

$1/3$ cup (80ml) lime juice

1 red thai chilli, seeded, chopped finely

$1/4$ cup coarsely chopped fresh coriander

Shell and devein prawns, leaving heads and tails intact. Combine prawns in large bowl with garlic, 2 tablespoons of the juice, half of the chilli and 1 tablespoon of the coriander, cover; stand 10 minutes. **Barbecue** (or grill or char-grill) prawns until just changed in colour. Serve prawns topped with combined remaining juice, chilli and coriander.

SERVES 4
Per serving 0.9g fat; 493kJ

crusted lamb
mini roasts

2 medium lamb mini roasts (700g)

1 tablespoon seeded mustard

2 teaspoons finely chopped fresh rosemary

2 teaspoons sea salt

Preheat oven to hot. Cook lamb in large heated oiled frying pan until browned all over. Place lamb on wire rack in baking dish; brush with mustard, sprinkle with combined rosemary and salt. **Bake** lamb, uncovered, in hot oven about 20 minutes or until cooked as desired. Cover lamb, rest 5 minutes; cut into thick slices just before serving.

SERVES 4
Per serving
6.4g fat; 849kJ

barbecued kebabs

and vegetables

*12 ready-made
beef kebabs*

*6 medium egg
tomatoes (450g),
halved lengthways*

*500g asparagus,
halved*

600g cup mushrooms

*125g sun-dried
tomato butter*

Barbecue (or grill
or char-grill) kebabs
for 5 minutes. Add
tomato, asparagus
and mushrooms;
cook until kebabs
and vegetables
are browned and
cooked as desired.
Brush kebabs and
vegetables with
sun-dried tomato
butter occasionally
during cooking.

SERVES 4
Per serving
53.1g fat; 3419kJ

glossary

antipasto char-grilled vegetables a bottled mixture of eggplant, zucchini and capsicum preserved in oil and herbs.

bacon rashers also known as slices of bacon; made from cured, smoked pork-side.

beef

mince: also known as ground beef.

scotch fillet steak: also known as beef rib-eye steaks.

spare ribs: long, narrow cut of meat taken from the lower portion of the ribs.

T-bone steak: sirloin steak with the bone in and fillet-eye attached.

bok choy also known as chinese white cabbage or pak choi; has mild mustard taste. Baby bok choy is also available.

breadcrumbs, packaged fine, crunchy, commercially purchased breadcrumbs.

butter use salted or unsalted ("sweet") butter; 125g is equal to one stick butter.

garlic: if not available commercially, stir two cloves crushed garlic into 250g butter.

sun-dried tomato: if not available commercially, stir 2 tablespoons finely chopped semi sun-dried tomatoes into 250g butter.

buttermilk low-fat cultured milk; has slightly sour taste.

cheese

bocconcini: small rounds of fresh "baby" mozzarella.

fetta: crumbly goat- or sheep-milk cheese; has salty taste.

goat: made from goat milk; has earthy taste. Available in soft and firm textures.

parmesan: sharp-tasting, dry, hard cheese.

pizza: commercial blend of processed grated cheddar, mozzarella and parmesan.

ricotta: sweet, fairly moist, fresh curd cheese.

chickpeas sandy-coloured legume, also known as channa or garbanzo.

chillies wear rubber gloves when seeding and chopping fresh chillies as they can burn your skin.

thai: range in colour from bright-red to dark-green and taste medium-hot.

chorizo sausage Spanish in origin; made of ground pork, garlic and chillies.

choy sum also known as flowering bok choy or flowering white cabbage.

coconut milk pure unsweetened coconut milk; available in cans.

couscous a fine, grain-like cereal; made from semolina.

cream (minimum fat content 35%) also known as pure cream and pouring cream.

sour: (minimum fat content 35%) a thick, commercially cultured soured cream.

dijonnaise if unavailable commercially, combine 2 teaspoons dijon mustard and ½ cup mayonnaise.

flour, plain an all-purpose flour, made from wheat.

ketjap manis Indonesian thick, sweet soy sauce.

lamb

cutlet: small, tender rib chop.

loin: row of eight ribs from the tender mid-section.

mini roasts (trim lamb round or topside): from the chump and leg, eye of loin and loin.

rack: row of cutlets.

mexicana chilli beans canned pinto beans with chilli.

noodles

rice stick: dried noodle made from rice flour.

hokkien: also known as stir-fry noodles; fresh, yellow-brown wheat-flour noodles.

udon: available fresh and dried; broad, white, Japanese wheat noodles.

oil

olive: mono-unsaturated; made from the pressing of tree-ripened olives.

peanut: pressed from ground peanuts; has high smoke point.

vegetable: any of a number of oils sourced from plants rather than animal fats.

onion

green: also known as scallion or (incorrectly) shallot; an immature onion, having a long, bright-green edible stalk.

red: also known as Spanish, red Spanish or Bermuda onion; a sweet-flavoured, large, purple-red onion.

pizza base commercially packaged pre-cooked wheat-flour round bases, sold in a variety of sizes.

plum sauce a thick, sweet and sour dipping sauce made from plums, vinegar, sugar, chillies and spices.

polenta a flour-like cereal made of ground corn (maize); coarse-textured cornmeal. Also the name of the dish made from it.

pork

fillet: skinless, boneless eye-fillet cut from the loin.

leg steak: schnitzel, usually cut from the leg or rump.

prawns also called shrimp.

rice, arborio large, round-grained rice, well-suited to absorbing cooking liquid.

rice wine sweet, golden wine made from fermented rice.

spinach leafy vegetable; often called english spinach or, incorrectly, silverbeet.

stock 1 cup (250ml) stock equals 1 cup (250ml) water plus 1 crumbled stock cube (or 1 tspn stock powder).

sugar, brown extremely soft, finely granulated sugar retaining molasses.

sukiyaki sauce bottled sauce from Japan; blend of sugar, soy sauce, mirin and salt.

tandoori paste Indian blend of hot and fragrant spices.

tartare sauce mayonnaise with added capers, spices and gherkins.

teriyaki marinade a blend of soy sauce, wine, vinegar and spices.

tomato

egg: also known as roma or plum tomatoes; small with an elongated shape.

paste: triple-concentrated tomato puree.

wasabi paste a fiery sauce based on Asian horseradish; traditionally served with Japanese raw fish dishes.

yogurt plain, unflavoured yogurt; can be used as a meat tenderiser, and as an enricher and thickener.

index

These conversions are approximate only, but the difference between an exact and the approximate conversion of various liquid and dry measures is minimal and will not affect your cooking results.

Measuring equipment
The difference between one country's measuring cups and another's is, at most, within a 2 or 3 teaspoon variance. (For the record, 1 Australian metric measuring cup holds approximately 250ml.) The most accurate way of measuring dry ingredients is to weigh them. For liquids, use a clear glass or plastic jug having metric markings.

Note: NZ, Canada, USA and UK all use 15ml tablespoons. Australian tablespoons measure 20ml.
All cup and spoon measurements are level.

How to measure
When using graduated measuring cups, shake dry ingredients loosely into the appropriate cup. Do not tap the cup on a bench or tightly pack the ingredients unless directed to do so. Level the top of measuring cups and measuring spoons with a knife. When measuring liquids, place a clear glass or plastic jug having metric markings on a flat surface to check accuracy at eye level.

Dry Measures

metric	imperial
15g	1/2oz
30g	1oz
60g	2oz
90g	3oz
125g	4oz (1/4lb)
155g	5oz
185g	6oz
220g	7oz
250g	8oz (1/2lb)
280g	9oz
315g	10oz
345g	11oz
375g	12oz (3/4lb)
410g	13oz
440g	14oz
470g	15oz
500g	16oz (1lb)
750g	24oz (1 1/2lb)
1kg	32oz (2lb)

We use large eggs having an average weight of 60g.

Liquid Measures

metric	imperial
30ml	1 fluid oz
60ml	2 fluid oz
100ml	3 fluid oz
125ml	4 fluid oz
150ml	5 fluid oz (1/4 pint/1 gill)
190ml	6 fluid oz
250ml (1cup)	8 fluid oz
300ml	10 fluid oz (1/2 pint)
500ml	16 fluid oz
600ml	20 fluid oz (1 pint)
1000ml (1litre)	1 3/4 pints

Helpful Measures

metric	imperial
3mm	1/8in
6mm	1/4in
1cm	1/2in
2cm	3/4in
2.5cm	1in
6cm	2 1/2in
8cm	3in
20cm	8in
23cm	9in
25cm	10in
30cm	12in (1ft)

Oven Temperatures
These oven temperatures are only a guide.
Always check the manufacturer's manual.

	°C (Celsius)	°F (Fahrenheit)	Gas Mark
Very slow	120	250	1
Slow	150	300	2
Moderately slow	160	325	3
Moderate	180 –190	350 – 375	4
Moderately hot	200 – 210	400 – 425	5
Hot	220 – 230	450 – 475	6
Very hot	240 – 250	500 – 525	7

at your fingertips

These elegant slipcovers store up to 10 mini books and make the books instantly accessible.

And the metric measuring cups and spoons make following our recipes a piece of cake.

Book Holder
Australia and overseas:
$A8.95 (incl. GST).

Metric Measuring Set
Australia: $6.50 (incl. GST).
New Zealand: $A8.00.
Elsewhere: $A9.95.
Prices include postage and handling.
This offer is available in all countries.

Photocopy and complete the coupon below

Mail or fax Photocopy and complete the coupon below and post to AWW Home Library Reader Offer, ACP Direct, PO Box 7036, Sydney NSW 1028, *or* fax to (02) 9267 4363.

Phone Have your credit card details ready, then, if you live in Sydney, phone 9260 0000; if you live elsewhere in Australia, phone 1800 252 515 (free call, Mon-Fri, 8.30am-5.30pm).

Australian residents We accept the credit cards listed on the coupon, money orders and cheques.

Overseas residents We accept the credit cards listed on the coupon, drafts in $A drawn on an Australian bank, and also British, New Zealand and U.S. cheques in the currency of the country of issue.

☐ **Book holder**   ☐ **Metric measuring set**
Please indicate number(s) required.

Mr/Mrs/Ms _____

Address _____

_____

Postcode _____ Country _____

Phone: Business hours ( ) _____

I enclose my cheque/money order for $ _____ payable to ACP Direct

OR: please charge $ _____ to my: ☐ Bankcard   ☐ Visa

☐ Amex   ☐ MasterCard   ☐ Diners Club   Expiry Date ___/___

Cardholder's signature _____

Please allow up to 30 days for delivery within Australia.
Allow up to 6 weeks for overseas deliveries. Both offers expire 31/12/02.
HLMTFIV01

Food editor Pamela Clark
Associate food editor Karen Hammial
Assistant food editor Kathy McGarry
Assistant recipe editor Elizabeth Hooper

HOME LIBRARY STAFF
Editor-in-chief Mary Coleman
Managing editor Susan Tomnay
Editor Julie Collard
Concept design Jackie Richards
Designer Ayesha Ali Raza
Book sales manager Jennifer McDonald
Group publisher Jill Baker
Publisher Sue Wannan
Chief executive officer John Alexander

Produced by *The Australian Women's Weekly* Home Library, Sydney.

Colour separations by
ACP Colour Graphics Pty Ltd, Sydney.
Printing by Dai Nippon Printing in Korea

Published by ACP Publishing Pty Limited, 54 Park St, Sydney; GPO Box 4088, Sydney, NSW 1028. Ph: (02) 9282 8618 Fax: (02) 9267 9438.

awwhomelib@acp.com.au
www.awwbooks.com.au

Australia Distributed by Network Distribution Company, GPO Box 4088, Sydney, NSW 1028. Ph: (02) 9282 8777 Fax: (02) 9264 3278.

United Kingdom Distributed by Australian Consolidated Press (UK), Moulton Park Busine Centre, Red House Road, Moulton Park, Northampton, NN3 6AQ. Ph: (01604) 497 531 Fax: (01604) 497 533 acpukltd@aol.com

Canada Distributed by Whitecap Books Ltd, 351 Lynn Ave, North Vancouver, BC, V7J 2C4, Ph: (604) 980 9852.

New Zealand Distributed by Netlink Distributio Company, Level 4, 23 Hargreaves St, College Hill, Auckland 1, Ph: (9) 302 7616.

South Africa Distributed by:
PSD Promotions (Pty) Ltd, PO Box 1175, Isando 1600, SA, Ph: (011) 392 6065; and CNA Limited, Newsstand Division, PO Box 107 Johannesburg 2000. Ph: (011) 491 7500.

Take 5 ingredients

Includes index.
ISBN 1 86396 248 4

1. Cookery.
I. Title: Australian Women's Weekly.
(Series: Australian Women's Weekly make it tonight mini series).
641.5

© ACP Publishing Pty Limited 2001
ABN 18 053 273 546

Cover: Pasta with salami and char-grilled vegetables, page 28.
Stylist: Anna Phillips
Photographer: Stuart Scott
Back cover: Tomato chilli prawns, page 16.